M000198078

"*Magnolia Canopy Otherworld* explores the places that hold the muddied and forested histories of women. Sensory and sensual, Erin Carlyle's poems portray an elemental girlhood, and the fragility and publicness of a body, even in the woods. These poems are full of dangerous baptisms, teeth and hooks, gothic flora and their attendant ghosts. Carlyle's style is lush and lovely, but always tugging with its dark undertow until we feel our own animal selves rise out at the end, gasping and human again."

— Traci Brimhall, author of *our lady of the ruins*

"Erin Carlyle's *Magnolia Canopy Otherworld* is a book of precise, gemlike images, where beneath the duende-soaked landscape of rivers, rabbits, trailers, and woodlots, the evidence of patriarchal damage lurks like an undertow. As an act of resistance, Carlyle sets before us the world we have been taught to ignore and says *look*: the roadkill, the small child wandering alone, the desolation of addiction, the woman-as-object. Wherever the poet casts her eye, the ghosts of violence, family, adolescence, and loss materialize and their visitations are traced with an urgent lyricism that is both gritty and graceful. Open these pages and watch as Erin Carlyle calls forward the drowned girls in their matching white dresses. Be ready for her to interrupt your life with poem after stunning poem in this haunting and arresting debut."

— F. Daniel Rzicznek, author of *Settlers*

"In this haunting and visceral collection, Carlyle guides us on an imaginative and transformative journey through Southern girlhood in which girls are ghosts, girls are animals, girls are daughters and lost friends, girls struggle to be more than just bodies. A riveting, smart, and unforgettable debut."

— Rebecca Morgan Frank, author of *Little Murders Everywhere*

MAGNOLIA CANOPY OTHERWORLD
Erin Carlyle

INDEPENDENTLY PUBLISHED BY
DRIFTWOOD   PRESS

Independently published by Driftwood Press
in the United States of America.

Managing Poetry Editor & Interviewer: Jerrod Schwarz
Cover Image: Neva Hosking
Cover Design: Sally Franckowiak
Interior Design & Copyeditor: James McNulty
Fonts: Maecenas, Sitka, Garamond, & Merriweather

First published December 15, 2020
ISBN-13: 978-1-949065-08-4

Please visit our website at www.driftwoodpress.net
or email us at editor@driftwoodpress.net.

For Shane and Frank
For Daddy

Contents

Family is family, but even love can't keep people from eating at each other.

— *Bastard out of Carolina*, Dorothy Allison, 1992

Sunday Drive

We drive in cold weather: three
in the front seat. Momma lays a hand

on my chest—a sudden stop. We pass over
a frozen bridge, and if I rise in my seat,

I can see down to the water, to the ice
where I know girls slip under and get fished out—

trash stuck on skirts. I know girls wait
there, but daddy drives

fast, and I see ditches along the side
of the road, and dogs, dead in winter,

dressed in leaves, their paws look
like hands. They're women in the blur

of his driving, dancing like wet, tangled hair.

Can't Stop Burning a Witch

We set a girl to burn,
and in the ruin of her body,

we stamp our feet—cake the mud
and ash. We set her to burn,

and we've been taught to hold
our tongue, to kill

that ancient stone-pit in our stomachs.
The mother yelled: *she is not a witch*

as her body was rolled
through the center of town,

and we thought, *Are we also dead?*
The other girls met hand to hand

as she lit up the night,
and we thought: *Is this all?*

An Egg Compulsion

1

We crack the egg, and the weak
animal comes out wanting.

It crawls before it walks, and we sing
to it as it moves up our arms.

When we were young we chased
each other in the fields. Before the egg,

our bodies were tender, our nipples
pert, but the house holds us captive

now, and our fathers told us to keep
our knees tight. They said:

listen to the sound of a needle.

2

My little girl is an idea in a golden egg.
The man brings me breakfast—I eat

her, she grows inside me. All little
children find their host, and the trick

is now on me. I could never say no
to the doubling process, and I split,

try to leave her in the woods, but she comes
for me, grows bigger than me, splits on her own,

becomes more than one little girl, blonde
and barefoot on the forest floor, and I beg

for mercy while they prepare the pot and fire.

Obedience

She says: *put your hand first*
to the ground,
and then to your heart.
Don't believe in god.

I ask: were we put
in charge by a beautiful,

suited man? If we add
bodies to the earth are we God—
worthy? She gives me

her fine hair, and I give it
back. We walk side
by side in thick pine, and look
for a cardinal.

(I am turning into a cardinal.)

We look for any bird left.

She reminds me her body
was once her own,
and now she shares it with me.

She gives me her hands.

Dressing Room

Salt cures the meat, and rubbing
makes it tender. I never forget

to examine the fresh animal kill
of my body. How the moon

pulls on me, makes me raw,
plucked chicken skin—the smell

of blood and herbs. I am
the eater, and I eat myself.

As soon as I came to being,
I ate. I learned: the meat-hook

is mandatory. I learned: my belly
folds, and I have a calorie

count. I am how a pig tastes.

The Slumber Party

I heard she went and died
into another girl, in a house

near a swamp where girls are caught
face down, muck deep, and motherless.

She told me there were other girls
sitting at a kitchen table with empty

plates in front of them,
and more girls in the bathroom

draped over the shower—wet. She asked:

What man made their bodies
into tables—arms and legs bent backward,

a coffee cup on the sternum? She didn't know
she would be used up, but she told me

she tip-toed through the rooms
tracing her name on the walls just in case.

My girl lost herself—a blonde hair flood
on the floor, and she came back to me

years later wound tight, a coil, said: *Why me?*

Tales

Your mother is calling
You from the top of a pine—
wind threatening her fall.
You were an egg, a stomach
ache, and then she dropped you
in a green muck—hatched
you, said: *Go be a woman.*

*

You are on a bed
he made of other women's
bodies. He tells you not
to look, but you can't
shut your eyes. He says:
When a girl is full grown,
you can have her, and she
will still be a girl.

*

Momma, she is still calling
you. She has followed the trail
of your teeth, but you're not
there. She doesn't know
what else to do.

*

Your momma taught you
how to catch an animal
and skin it. You only
have to wait for it.

*

In the belly of a bear,
you drink tea and eat
your own arm. You never
even try to get out,
just keep eating.

Two Girls

I pulled my shirt off in woods
that smelled dank and old, but I knew

it was planted only a few years
before I was born. It was a passage—

a rite for me to pull your hand up
to my newly grown breasts. All around

the trees rumored, and when I got
to school the next day, I could hear

the whisper of my arched back and the red
clay mud and both of us coming of age.

*

At night the dream of your body lying
in the woods gets mixed up with the dream

of you kissing me at a party. I try
to get your bones off the ground before

the dogs get us both, but they circle
and growl and I can't find the place

where your mouth should be. I can't
say your name loud enough. Down

the path before us, your mother closes
the door to your house and the light

from the windows looks like a forest
fire. This is what it's like to love you.

Girl, Dirt, and Wall
For Francesca Woodman

Your body is a scratched photograph,
and I want to live like you do

in front of a ruined wall, buttons on my skirt
begging to be opened. You hold a jewel

behind your back, palmed in your hand,
and there are so many white ash

trees behind you. I want to be in your photo.
I want to put a mirror under my naked

body, and a finger in my mouth.
I see myself like you on the floor

—stretch-marked. My dirty feet over
yours. The tiles under your body are old—

you are not. You are only nineteen living
in Italy. When I was nineteen, I lived with a man,

did his dishes, and I have never been
to Italy. You sit with your hands over your mouth—

back straight, head down. The floor under you
is celled—a honeycomb, and I would do your dishes.

Francesca, now your head is on the floor,
your feet are shelved inside a cabinet,

and there is no room for your arms.
If you were married, this is where you

would put your china, says the stuffed raccoon
at your ear. I hear you whisper

to the cabinet: *a curio is only for body
curiosities.* You cannot close the cabinet,

and there isn't room for me inside.
Look, three women who are also you hide

behind mirrors—their own reflection.
Am I also there in the blur of those bodies,

or am I in the mold on the walls?
What it comes down to is your dull stare

and your birth certificate. Am I there
in your gaze? I hover over the little fish

in your bathtub, and there is the light coming
in the windows. In all that sparkling doom

and your back to the camera, did you expect me
to pick up your book? I try to figure the blurs

of your long exposure and your suicide,
and how I came after you, still a woman,

and in your shadow, I try to master my body.

Franklin, Kentucky 1995

My grandma is in her living room in a polyester
dress suit. She fills green glass bowls with full-

shelled nuts while my brothers and I watch
music videos on her console television.

Beside me my middle brother opens and closes
the corkscrew on his Swiss Army Knife.

A fog blows out of the pink bathroom down
the hall, and covers the picture frames.

My kindergarten photo goes first,
and then Grandma's momma and her sister

beside an old car, and then my daddy
and momma stoic in front of a trailer. The fog

erases her pink shag runner, and the closet door.
It's coming for us. It covers the T.V., spreads

up the walls and over the wood paneling. I slip
between the sofa and the coffee table,

and pray to the Pinky and Blue Boy on the living
room wall—it erases them. My grandma

says something important, but I half hear her,
and she's gone before fog rolls us all over.

Momma as Death and Gate Keeper

She is a white pill

now, suspended in thin air,

and I hear her say she hopes

to come back down, hit

the ground, and grow

her body into a pine tree,

tall, alone. I say: I'd climb

you, knock your only cones

to the ground where the dirt

will swallow the seeds,

but I'm no arborist.

I just know how

to pick a tree clean,

and I know how to let

the death of it burst

inside me like the green

unraveling of the kudzu.

On the Horizon of Recollection

A circle of women in the creek
raise you up, their skirts a white blur
in the water—milk. This is a not a baptism,
but a call back to your life after you crawled
out of the cave of your mother,
that old danger. Now walk down
the dirt road and find the outhouse.
Is your grandmother there in her polyester
pants and floral button up top—a beer can
in her hand? A man next to her helps you
sit on the toilet, and a horse is standing
in the field across the way. A red-haired boy
says you can't feed it. The horse blows air
out of its nostrils—you jump. Is there a prisoner
down past the woods, or is it just some man
working on the road? He blocks the cars,
and your daddy honks, mad. Your uncle
is at the base of the tree. He lifts you up to pull
Spanish moss down from a branch. You weave
a nest and put little white pebbles in it.
At the door of the trailer, your father holds
a carving knife, and you smell animal in the air.

My momma cuts virgin switches with her gums,

because the stars at night are her teeth,
rotted out of her mouth one at a time.

My momma believes that god is judge, and the man
who dragged her body into the woods

wasn't her husband. I just laugh at her tears
and wait for my turn in the pine. Her face

is the sunken-cheeked moon. I whisper my fears
to her, and she tells me her lungs aren't black,

but they orbit the southern sun like planets. At night
she stays up on the couch burning holes

in a blanket when she nods off. My momma
always snaps her neck up quick because she fears

she won't wake. She calls the doctor at the pain clinic.
He takes her money, helps her stop chewing

her fingers. My momma counts all the pills,
and when I feel my monthly blood, she hands me one.

The Animal

The Animal walks
on the hot sidewalk barefoot.

It wears a sundress
with straps that tie into bows

on each shoulder, and it steps
over branches that have fallen

to the road. A stick pierces
through the meat of the Animal's

foot, and it yells out for someone

else's mother to help it, sings
a song to mend the broken

skin. The Brother rides by
on his bike and laughs.

      *

The Animal wakes and thinks
it dreamed of the Hello Kitty Store.

It smells food in the kitchen,
but isn't sure where

the kitchen is. At the foot
of the couch where it slept—

empty beer cans and the Uncle—
still sleeping.

*

When it first notices
blood on its panties

it is disturbed that
it isn't red.

Instead a thick
brown clotted mess falls

out, and The Momma
says to get a pad.

The Animal fears
that everyone can

smell it. It takes
longer and longer

to finish a bath.

*

A girl from school
asks it to play sex.

They roll around
on her bed. One

is the boy
and one is the girl.

*

At a party The Uncle pins
it down to play.

He says it looks
too much like

The Momma. This is
the night it hears

Abbey Road
for the first time.

*

In the middle
of the night, The Animal

hears The Uncle
ask The Momma what

her bra looks like.
Outside in the van,

The Daddy sleeps
off too many beers.

The Animal is stuck
on the couch, head

under the covers,
listening to them

kiss. In its head
it sings the entire

medley from the
second side of the record.

*

The Animal pulls
the stick from its foot

slowly. A woman
from across the street

brings it her slippers
to wear. It walks

home struggling
to keep them on,

blood seeping
through the sole.

       *

There is a wild
dog following

The Animal home
from school.

The dog smells
the musty blood

between The Animal's
legs. When it weaves

the dog weaves, so it stops
still and just waits.

Grandma, I want to go down to Mrs. Ruby's

where I will lay myself over a chair
in her backyard. I don't know if you can
see me, but there is blood
from the root of me here with Ruby
and all her neighbors' trailers. My brother
is swinging from her tire swing,
and I push him, push through him.
It's always December in Alabama. I smell
the smoke from the fire ring. It's for me.
I called it forth from my memory,
and then I see my child self in her blue
Christmas dress. She's going to be in a play
tonight. I want to tell her something.
I want to tell her I love her, but she's gone
inside for some cookies, and my brother
goes too, and there are sentinels on both
sides of the door. Macramé hanging plant
holders with little dried June bugs hooked
down the yarn, white husks.

Must Leave Something

Smoke from a darling
body rises into an Alabama

night. She lets all her bones
go, but never dances

around fire. It's too hard
for people to hear about

the dog killed on the side
of the road, so her mouth stops

dead. She thinks to herself:
Call Momma every day, drive

the car, sweep the kitchen floor
because the wind outside

is loud. It cuts the corner

of her house, makes animal
sounds, and when she cooks

for her husband or puts herself
to bed, the wind says *grieve*.

Doctor Shopping Ghost Story

The doctors I see are benevolent spirits
filling my prescriptions, orange bottles

awaiting blessing—for a doctor to dip
a pen and anoint the paper. I hand one

doctor my pain, another my worry. I fill
out the paperwork, present it to their open arms.

The doctors watch me shiver. They write
their diagnosis on my spine—whisper me

back into being. Give me what I need, priests,
or I will seek until I become a Percocet ghost

haunting a body, holes for eyes—a sheet
soaked in Oxycontin, and you can never cut

me off. In the beginning it was
not about becoming a ghost—a transparent

pill casing empty, longing. In the beginning
I was flat on my back looking up at the stars.

The Animal in Training

The Animal loves it when
The Daddy gets back, but The Momma

tells it that when it was small
The Daddy came home freshly shaven

after a week of hauling,
and the Animal didn't know

who he was, cried when he held
it. This time The Daddy

brings the Animal powder compacts,
but they're the wrong shade.

The Animal opens one,
sees its reflection in the mirror.

It puts two compacts in its backpack,
and at school girls take turns

with the mirror, caress
their faces with the puffs inside,

and they don't press hard enough,
no make-up goes on their faces,

but they keep practicing.

*

The Animal is tired and ready
for bed. It crawls up the bunk bed

it shares with The Brother.
The Daddy says that it will need

its own bedroom soon,
and what The Animal doesn't know

is that in four years it will be sixteen
and that will make it ready

to consent. It does not know
consent is an act of speech

and not the body. It doesn't know
any of that. At eleven

it has just given up its Barbies,
and it wants a Sgt. Pepper jacket

for Christmas, the one that George wears.
It hopes The Momma will get someone

to sew it, and it doesn't want
to have its own bedroom,

doesn't want to miss The Brother.
It doesn't know that at sixteen, The Brother

will walk in on it changing,
and he'll let out a frightened sigh.

                    *

The Animal walks the deep
woods looking for sticks to crack,

rocks to throw. It is almost twelve,
sings "Nights in White Satin"

in its head. It wears too-tight jeans,
and a white training bra under its T-shirt.

The bra rubs against its budding
breasts, makes The Animal wince.

The Animal sees magazine pages
strewn around the trees. It isn't unusual

for men to sleep in these woods,
and it has seen a tent or two.

The Animal walks over to a skinny
pine tree, reaches down, picks up a *Playboy*

page: a woman, naked, arms up
in pose, and another image stuck

to the back, more women, more poses.
The Animal folds the pictures, pushes

them in its pocket,
opens the button on its jeans

to make room for its belly,
immediate relief. It walks

through the woods collecting women.

The President Declared a Public Health Emergency

but the pain clinic is alive and it wants to bring its children in close. It whispers: *come here, come here little one* then hands my mother her prescriptions. In devotion she sits up sleeping—letting out her muscles. She doesn't move— body shrinking. My mother gladly gives up her bones. The clinic suckles my mother's breast but then tells her it is her mother. It is her grave-chair—her body-ache. My mother invites me in. She warns me that we will forever throw up and shiver our deaths without the clinic. In its waiting room we pass pills fist to fist while it creatures around us like love.

Replay

I go under—a tulip dipped.

My spilled-milk

dress spreads around me

and does anyone send a net out

to catch me, to pull me to the surface?

I'm in the water, and in my memory

moving around the aching land

where my grandmother once

lived. I see her in her nightgown,

feel her hand—a jolt to my face—

the pain, her hand—

a cold compress, and I feel

the land, the land where she lived,

Spanish moss hanging

from the trees. She puts

me to bed in a pile

of leaves. Where is my mother?

Behind her trailer, behind god's

house? I slide down the grey dirt

hill to the river, ask

an alligator for safe passage,

and a bird of paradise flies

above my head, says

something I don't understand.

Come out of the dream, out

of the water. The moon above me

pulls some tide inside me. It remembers

me and remembers my mother

flicking a cigarette into a fire pit.

Dead Things

Once a cat climbed into my lap
in a parking lot, and I kept her
company while she died.

In my ear, I thought she said:
I don't know what is happening,

but maybe she really said something
about falling into a river,
or about sleeping under a porch.

I thought: I've never helped anyone
die before. Where do I get a brick?
Where do I find a shoebox

at this time of night? I thought
of the time my brother told me
that birds only feel one emotion—anger.

This was after I pulled an egg
out of a nest, but I never killed a thing.

Spells Cast on the Animal

Potion: Sitting on a coffee table
at The Grandmother's house

is an ashtray, a burning cigarette,
and a can of Budweiser.

The Animal sips the beer
while its grandmother is cleaning.

Later The Grandmother will stop
drinking. The Daddy and The Uncle

will think she's judging
them. The Grandmother will tell

them she doesn't want it in her house.
She will not let the Grandfather buy

any beer at the store. The Daddy will say
she thinks she's better than him.

*

Incantation: The Animal is trying to sleep
but it can't because the music is too loud.

The Momma and Daddy are talking
about how The Rolling Stones

were much darker than The Beatles,
and The Uncle is slur-voiced, singing.

The Animal walks into the room,
and the Momma tells her to go

the fuck to bed. The Animal, tiny
and sleepy, sits down between

The Momma's legs, and starts to sing,
It will go to school the next day tired.

*

Levitation: At a party The Animal hopes
to see a boy. It is sixteen. It is following
a friend around so that it won't
have to be on its own. It doesn't talk

to anyone, wrings its hands behind its back.
It drinks beer out of nervousness. When offered

a white pill the Animal takes it with its drink,
and it starts to itch and float.

There is a queasy turn in its stomach,
and it stumbles around. The teenagers laugh,

and float and itch as well. The Animal's
eyes are heavy-lidded. It finds a room to sleep.

Root Canal

Down the dark
hole of my cavity
you can see vines

strangling rusted cars,
and there's an alligator
waiting on the river

bank—see his jaws
slam down on my sweet,
lost beagle. If a girl

puts Spanish moss
on her head like hair,
is she then a grown woman,

asks the man in the trailer
park who watches me
ride my bike. In oppressive

humidity, I bathe
in a storm drain
puddle. At dusk,

I examine my body.
The tiny lump breasts

hurt to touch, and boys come
by, tell me to open

my mouth and take
their sour-breathed kisses.

The In-Between

Here is a story: My mother
saves me from the electric

pull of the kitchen. She travels
to the otherside to find me

in pink, asleep, and followed
by the dead. She carries me

home, teaches me how
to dial a psychic phone.

I call my grandmother,
god. Her voice is muffled

by mud. I tracked it into her
house. I'm sorry, I stamped it under

my shoes. I walk down the road,
to her house where rain

has made a pool in her backyard.
The neighbors meet in that hole

in the ground, make O's
with their mouths at an ancient

tree. I think: How do I get my grandmother
out? The tree swallows me

down its trunk stomach, and I hear
a man sing *God is in his holy temple*

as I fall through a static-somewhere.

Girls Who Ride Horses

In red ribbon bows and exposed
thighs, they circle on the gym court,

and then we watch them put on
expensive jackets, slip them down soft,

young shoulders. They are our white
smile in the hall, our secret hand to hand

pass of tampons and cigarettes. We see
them walk like sleep in short, pink

skirts while deep down their pretty gardens
are awake. Oh quiet girl in class—

pencil breaks, her red face. Go up to the front
while they watch from the back. We think:

what will we do without the pretty girls?

We play their game. We ask: please, conjure
us all, rip our papers in half, hand us our fates.

When asked for a story

The girl wanders away

She is lost. She thinks
of her mother, fat
and cooking at the stove.

Her mother whipped
her dirty dish cloth
over her shoulder and said:

It's time for dinner.

*

And finds herself in a clearing

She doesn't know
what to do about the thick

blood between her legs,
but she could tell you more

about the moment she cracked
her head against a rock,

and how the blood took a long
time to make its way down her face.

*

She thinks back further in her memory.

On the bathroom floor,
her mother vomits foam

from an ulcer. The other hungry
wolf cubs lie still

at her mother's feet,
and she just got

up and wiped her face.

*

How could she ever make it home?

This is what she would like for you
to remember: a quick beating heart,

a mother nursing, a lion in the middle
of a freeway, a little girl smiling.

Post-Eve

You are tender when you say to me:
pull this bone out of my body.

If you throw me out
with the trash. I'll leave,

get this bone appraised—take
it to pawn. My feet one

in front of the other. My head,
as it should be, downcast.

See the bone in my hand,
I will get nothing for it—

won't be worth the walk,
so I stick the bone inside me. I lie

down on the asphalt road, and listen
to distant men—they yell

my name. I pull my skin apart,
recite a story: *My father was once a tree.*

True Crime

We listen to her nipple-cut
and her blood. Hear the dirt where

she's buried, and her deep
secret. If you put your knuckles in

that ground, and turn your fist
like a key, you can open

a magnolia canopy otherworld
where she lives with teeth marks

and her hair a mess in plastic
wrap cover. We have a dead

women obsession. The girls
all freckled and water-wrinkled.

The low woods hold
their memories— belly-cuts.

Listen to them. Pull back
the mist. Help them climb

over the bone scatter of time.

Sunken

The Rivermen pull a woman up from the water. It's
you, Jenny. They count your limbs before they zip. I
watch from my living room. I mouth: *oh my god* at
the screen while I eat cherry vanilla ice cream. I
wonder if you sensed something wrong before he
came over, or if you told someone where you'd be
that night. You say something through my TV—a
whisper in static. I tilt my head listening for words,
drop my spoon in melted pink.

* *

It's night at the river. The Rivermen want to catch animal bodies. They scour the bottom for her. Did she fall to the floor in her black bag dress—a hand push from the bank? The Rivermen are here to collect. They want to carry her up one piece at a time. We call her back to the surface. Momma's voice—a bell: *come back to me girl.*

* *

We walked alone in the woods, and I saw them before you did. The red-winged birds flew down from their forest canopy, and I told you how they come down to look for a mate—for a woman. Jenny, I remembered when we brushed each other's hair and drank from your mother's vodka, your hair a blonde mess—rats.

* *

I walk to meet my man—early night. We take a drive to the banks of the Chattahoochee. I have   never fished at night. We get our gear and walk to the edge of the water. He puts the bait on for me. He throws in my line. He says: *we will catch these fish. We will eat their bodies.*

* *

I'm thinking of you now, Jenny. The way your hands slid into your back pockets. The way you'd push me down. The way you brushed my hair, put red butterfly clips on each side. We are not girls anymore. I'm on your bank. There's a fish jumping in the distance.

* *

I'm falling to the floor and all I can think of are his hands. What could I do about his hands? He said: *Darling, Darling,* and I came here for him. After all, I came here for him.

* *

The Rivermen dive. Their nets cut tiny squares on the water. We dream they pull her out lung first. We dream her hair catches little fish for us to fry. On the banks dogs run hungry. Back and forth—noses to ground. A man shouts orders. The dogs catch a scent just before the water. Momma tosses coins, an offering like in church.

* *

Jenny, I remember when we talked about rich girls, and how we wanted something good like them. We wanted to grow up out of our pain. We wanted to find each other again after so many years, but how can I find you at the bottom of the river? I don't blame you. I think of you now as a ripple—a stone fallen through the center.

* *

The Rivermen give up their boats, gone from the water. I disintegrate—warped mind. I'm an Alabama shad—silver. I hide under rocks, my old skin picked clean.

＊ ＊

A Riverman shouts, and I can hear him. I can hear his dogs are hungry. Momma, a message: *men send other men into the water.* Mussel shells pull my hair, and I grow out of my dress. They want to pull me out lung first. Want to try to fry my fish. Momma tosses coins, and they scatter at the bottom. When the boats are all gone, animals rummage. I never come back.

My Cannibal

Out at the edge of the creek, a man tells me
he cannot be whole without the full body

of a woman. He wants to eat me up—a dog
and a bone. He wants me to invite him through

my silk, southern land to the hidden whole of me.
There is a danger in letting a man work me

until I'm done, and I don't understand
what it means to believe his fever, but he tells

me what he wants to hear and I slip my skin down
into the green muck. Once he has it, I walk into

the water—unborn and unwombed. A woman given
to desire. A woman entered deep in the belly

of his deepest birthday wish. When I'm gone,
he will think he is bigger than he ever could be.

Rabbit Diptych

I am the rabbit from my heart tied up
by the legs. You can break my skin:

bunch it around my ankles—twist.
Pull my fur until I'm raw. Is your knife big

enough? Do you see my ex-husbands
asleep in the bushes outside my apartment?

They dyed my feet blue for luck. I have to put
a quarter in a toy machine and hope they pop

back out. I know my career is my body,
but I am disappointed because my hunter

will not speak to me. Instead he whispers
sorrys to the wind while I sit in his hotel room.

*

You looked at me as if you already knew
you'd be pulling my fur from your teeth all night—

slack-jawed, salivating. When you pulled out
the white wine and not the red, I didn't understand

you knew what to pair me with. You hurried me
through my chewing. You didn't let me finish

my meal. The first time you pushed your fingers
through my thin membrane, I was not sure how

to react. The second time my body moistened
and opened. I even fell face-first into your lap.

I wondered which part of me would be a trophy,
or when you would give up and call me a cab.

Skinny Dipping

We girls love to dip our toes

in green creek water while we look

at boys through a fog veil,

and those boys look

at us half-cocked, want us

small. Do we like it? Do we want

to take our clothes off, go all the way

in the water—disappear, sirens

in scum? The boys play fight

in grey dirt—young dogs.

They don't pay us

any mind. We hold our noses, go down,

and our bodies come together,

—a silver fish,

beautiful like a coin. We swim

through crushed beer cans,

and picnic trash. When we come

out human again, we gasp for air.

The Afterlife of Women

For me to stay here with the dead
      I have to eat a flesh meal, make

the commitment, but for now I'm a struck
      chord. I sound through pine woods,

and the thick clay mud of Kentucky. We were all
      once girls here, wanted to experience

otherworlds, but now I can't find a woman
      here among the discarded diaries

and pocketbooks. In this place
      we all linger then disintegrate.

I think I smell the oldest
      danger in the air—magnolia on the wind.

I think I hear my mother calling: *get home.*

Magnolia Canopy Otherworld **is a collection that heavily focuses on people's relationship to place. Specifically, this collection opens up an expansive breadth of family dynamics, drilling deep into how poverty in the American South complicate those dynamics. What was the hardest and easiest parts of conveying this complex geography?**

In a sense, writing these poems came easy in that this was my lived experience as a child, though, you know, the artistic version of events. The people and the relationships in the poems are all based on real people, and in that same respect the landscape, the places, the water, and the trees were all based on Alabama and Kentucky, where I grew up. These are the places and people that come to me in my dreams. They influenced who I am as a person and as a poet. The hard part of writing this book was thinking of the feelings of the very real people that I based some of the work on. In order to be honest, I had to write about some really painful events and unfortunate circumstances. For instance, I don't shy away from writing about the effect that the Opioid crisis had on my family. We lost my father in August of 2019 from an overdose mixed with his heart condition. It's because of events like these that I don't think I mince words about my feelings on growing up in this kind of environment, though I do make sure to keep from placing the blame solely on my parents. When I was a teenager, it was hard for me to understand just how much my father was preyed upon by doctors and the pharmaceutical companies after his first heart attack at thirty-six. I hope that in this book I'm providing a more rounded view of the pain and ultimate sacrifice my father (and people like him) gave to the pharmaceutical companies. Still, I feel it is my right to be honest about my experiences though I don't want anyone I love to feel pain or embarrassment after reading this book. Everything I write is meant with love.

Throughout the collection, the speaker is often cloaked in a pseudo-persona called simply "the Animal." What were you able to communicate through this stand-in speaker that you would not have been able to otherwise?

The Animal is a little beast just trying to navigate life. It's kind of like an aerial view or a storybook version of events. This was one of the first poems I wrote for this book and it ended up being a trilogy that encapsulates the many themes of the book. I look at it as a way of taking the capital "I" out of the work. It's like a nature documentary.

This is something many poets grapple with—the confessional "I" and the limits it can have on a poem or collection. What are the advantages of shifting this point of view to something more animalistic? What are the disadvantages?

The Animal has to learn on her own. She's not a specific animal, but she represents that primal part of the "I." My sister-in-law is a fantastic artist, and she is currently making a short film for the "The Animal." She is interested in factory farming and conservation, so her interpretation of the poem has a lot to do with the cruelty we inflict on animals. To me, this is an apt interpretation; though when I started writing the series, I was mainly referring to my own feelings of vulnerability as a child. I guess in that way it's a bit more "confessional" than it seems. The animal has never been taught how to deal with a world that determines for her how her life is going to play out.

One of my favorite repeating moments in this collection is the constant return to woods and water, to natural geographies that are often twisted with dangers and uncertainty. When you set out to write *Magnolia Canopy Otherworld*, did you know that these natural elements would be a large focus of the collection? Did any parts of this landscape feel more or less important to include?

Yes, I did know that these natural elements would be a big part of the book. I've seen nature written as a serene place to experience god. My version of nature is uncertain and scary, a portal to an otherworld where memory lingers. I spent a lot of time in the woods as a child, and my grandmother lived on a big piece of land down a dirt road in a little town called Pittsview, Alabama. Her land had huge trees with Spanish moss hanging down, and behind her trailer there was a drop off that led to a body of water. I remember feeling both safe and afraid at her house. I often thought about falling down into the water or being eaten by an alligator. I think the experiences I had there are bound up with the land as described in the book.

Writing from the perspective of childhood, even our own

childhoods, is never an easy task, but these poems walk the fine line between revelatory wonder and sobering hindsight. Was writing from this perspective a challenge, or did it come naturally? In a poem, what can we learn from childhood that adulthood (or even adolescence) cannot communicate?

It came naturally in that I've been working on communicating these themes for a long time. I recently went back and read some of my (very terrible) teenage poetry. Even then I was trying to communicate the connection between poverty and the land, and the ways in which families traumatize each other. I like that you say "sobering hindsight" because as a woman in her late 30s, I can connect the dots a little better than I could at sixteen. I have empathy for the people who I was born to and who I grew up around. It's as if I have the chance to give that perspective to my younger self through poetry.

I think this is probably a common feeling for most writers, the queasiness of looking over our adolescent writing. That being said, is there anything from teenage poems that you still cherish or appreciate?

Of course! I love that I can look back on them and see the potential. I had to grow up pretty fast because of my family life, so I was tackling some really big issues in my poetry, but I was still a child. I think it's interesting to have a time capsule of that moment in my development as a person and as an artist.

The collection ends with an extended section on a drowned woman and the "Rivermen" who find her. Haunting and almost fable-like, these poems seem to culminate in the most horrifying of possibilities that were hinted at throughout earlier poems. Did you plan for this series of poems to appear at the end of *Magnolia Canopy Otherworld?* How does this exploration of death work in tandem with the end of the collection?

The Magnolia Canopy Otherworld is a place where the dead linger and float. I always thought there were probably women at the bottom of the Chattahoochee, or Nolan Lake in Kentucky, or any creek or river I visited. I don't know who put that in my head, or if it comes from watching too much *Unsolved Mysteries* with my mom. I just think that life is fleeting, and wherever you walk is somewhere someone else, long dead, was at some point, alive, and though I'm not a doomist, human beings aren't that nice to each other sometimes. When you're a woman, you know this. When you're poor, you know this. The Rivermen just do their job like anyone else. I don't know if I planned for it appearing at the end, but I did plan for it to work with the other poems in this section.

A lot of my childhood was spent in poor, rural farmlands too, and your explanation of callousness and how the Rivermen are "just do[ing] their jobs like anyone else" feels so true to that lifestyle. What, if any, are the hardest aspects of poverty to communicate in a poem? What aspects felt the easiest?

I guess it's easy for people to understand that poverty is hard on families, but the hardest part for me to communicate is that instability changes you as a child and you carry that with you into adulthood even if you have money.

How long had you been working on this collection? What poems, structures, or ideas didn't make it into the final manuscript, and why were they cut?

I've been working on this for a long time. I'm not a prolific writer and I retool things over and over, so it took me a couple of years to write *MCO*. There were a lot of random bits of "noise" in my head that got cut. I have scraped fragments of images that I'm constantly trying to put into poems. For instance, I wanted to write a poem about my dad. Before he died I had an image of him pulling me up from the water when I fell into a drop off as a little girl. It never worked, and when he died I pulled it up and tried to rework it, but then it became too saccharine because I was in a very utopian mind frame about him. As far as structure, I will work a line to death, so I have to step away before it dies. For the most part, I like a line to stand on its own if it can, or if it makes sense.

For aspiring poets reading this interview, how do you know when a line feels (if this is possible) done and ready? What is important about stepping away from the line?

That's my eternal dilemma. I think at some point you just have to step away. If you come back later and still feel okay, then it's ready. That's what I tell myself anyway.

Where does *Magnolia Canopy Otherworld* stand in the scope of your writing? Is this collection indicative of your poetry as a whole or do those poems hold a unique place in your personal catalogue?

I'd say that ten years ago my work was a bit angrier. I like to joke that I learned to tone down the metal. This is my debut collection, so I would say that this is a snapshot of what I am like as a poet right now, though I am moving to other topics and themes. I don't want to keep writing the same set of poems in twenty years.

This is an unknowable question, but what kind of poems would you like to be writing in twenty years?

I don't really know. Now that I think about it, I just want to be writing anything in twenty years. That should probably be the new goal: keep writing!

These poems never shy away from complex subject matter like adolescent sexuality, drug abuse, and poverty. What advice would you have for other poets working with similar or equally harrowing themes?

You have to write what you have to write, and if it's something that feels true to you, explore it. Just because something is difficult doesn't mean that you should shy away from it. Sometimes the most difficult things to write are the most worthwhile things to write.

For these poems specifically, what were some of your biggest artistic inspirations?

I was inspired by a lot of poets while writing this book such as Frank Stanford, Traci Brimhall, Sarah Rose Nordgren, and Sharon Olds. Sharon Olds' *The Dead and the Living* is amazing! I'm also very inspired by musicians like Tori Amos, Pj Harvey, Kate Bush, and Joanna Newsom. The poem "Replay" has a subtle nod to Kate Bush's "Hello Earth" from Hounds of Love. As for films, I connected with the work of Marielle Heller, especially *Diary of a Teenage Girl*, Ingmar Bergman's *Fannie and Alexander* and *Persona*, and Neil Jordan's *The Company of Wolves*. The poem "The In-between" is a fever dream mixture of the film *Poltergeist* and the time my grandmother's back yard flooded. Also, Jenny in "Sunken" is a bit of a wink to James Wright's "To the Muse."

What are you working on now? Any new projects in the

works?

I am at the beginning of a new project. I was swindled by a medium after my dad died, so I've been really interested in mediums and contacting the dead (no offense to any mediums reading this). It'll take some time to form, I'm sure.

This already sounds intriguing! How do you think this new collection will differ or evolve past *Magnolia Canopy Otherworld?*

I'm doing some research for this new project which is something sort of new for me, but the new work still has connections to *MCO*, though, in that some of my new poems come from my experience with grief over the death of my father. I'm not religious or spiritual, but the idea that someone can just stop existing is baffling. I don't know if the work will stay on that path though.

ACKNOWLEDGEMENTS

First, I want to say thank you to the editors at *Driftwood Press* for believing in my work. I couldn't have asked for a better publisher. I want to send my deepest gratitude and respect to my mentors and fellow poets Rebecca Morgan Frank, F. Daniel Rzicznek, and Abigail Cloud. Thank you for respecting my vision and helping me with multiple drafts of this book. I also want to send a special thank you to my high school English teacher and friend, Larissa Haynes. Thank you for reading my teenage poetry and taking it seriously and for taking me to my first Tori Amos concert. Thank you to The Cat Ladies, Rebecca Hoffman, my poetry cohorts and classmates, and to all of my friends, and an extra huge thank you to my husband, Shane Snyder. I couldn't have asked for a better partner (and editor). Lastly, I want to send love my family. It's been a hard ride, but we love each other anyway. Rest-in-Peace, Daddy.

Many thanks to the following journals and magazines where these poems first appeared, some in slightly different forms:

"On the Horizon of Recollection" *New South*, 2020
"Dead Things" & "The Slumber Party" *Pretty Owl Poetry*, 2020
"Momma as Death and Gatekeeper" & "Must Leave Something"
    Cagibi, 2020
"Two Girls," "My Cannibal" *Prairie Schooner*, 2020
"Girl, Dirt, Wall" & "The In-between" *Poetry South*, 2019
"Girls Who Ride Horses" & "The Afterlife of Women"
    Bateau Press, 2019
"Franklin, KY 1995" *American Literary Review*, 2019
"Can't Stop Burning a Witch" *Hawaii Pacific Review*, 2019
"An Egg Compulsion" *Ruminate*, 2019
"Rabbit Diptych" *Muse/A Journal*, 2019
"Root Canal" & "A Series of Tales" *The Hunger*, 2019
"Post-Eve" *2River View*, 2018
"My momma cuts virgin switches with her gums"
    Dream Pop Press, 2018
"The President Declared a Public Health Emergency" & "True Crime"
    Driftwood Press, 2018
"Doctor Shopping Ghost Story" *Counterclock*, 2018
"Dressing Room" *Turnip Truck(s)*, 2018

Erin Carlyle is a poet whose work is rooted in the American South. As a child she lived in Alabama along the Chattahoochee River, and at twelve she moved with her family to the cave country of South Central Kentucky. She holds a MFA in poetry from Bowling Green State University and currently lives with her husband and cat in Sacramento, California.

CPSIA information can be obtained
at www.ICGtesting.com
Printed in the USA
JSHW010255100920
7746JS00002B/168